<The Power of CODING/>

The Power of Ruby

Rachel Keranen

Cavendish Square
New York

Published in 2018 by Cavendish Square Publishing, LLC
243 5th Avenue, Suite 136, New York, NY 10016

Copyright © 2018 by Cavendish Square Publishing, LLC

First Edition

Library of Congress Cataloging-in-Publication Data

Names: Keranen, Rachel.
Title: The power of Ruby / Rachel Keranen.
Description: New York : Cavendish Square Publishing, 2018. | Series: The power of coding | Includes bibliographical references and index.
Identifiers: ISBN 9781502634184 (pbk.) |ISBN 9781502629500 (library bound) | ISBN 9781502629517 (ebook)
Subjects: LCSH: Ruby (Computer program language)--Juvenile literature. | Object-oriented programming (Computer science)--Juvenile literature. | Computer programming--Juvenile literature.
Classification: LCC QA76.73.R83 K43 2018 | DDC 005.133--dc23

Editorial Director: David McNamara
Editor: Caitlyn Miller
Copy Editor: Rebecca Rohan
Associate Art Director: Amy Greenan
Designer: Christina Shults
Production Assistant: Karol Szymczuk

Printed in the United States of America

\

<Chapter One/>

The History of Ruby

In 1993, Yukihiro Matsumoto created a programming language that would shape the future of web development. Matsumoto, who goes by the nickname Matz, was a programmer working for a Japanese software company at the time. From a young age, Matz had dreamed of creating his own programming language. When he fulfilled that dream with Ruby, he created a language that today is used by companies around the world. Twitter, for example, was originally built using Ruby, and companies like Groupon and Kickstarter were built and continue to run on Ruby today.

Opposite: Ruby is written in a user-friendly way that reads very much like English

The language is known for being programmer friendly and for emphasizing the happiness and productivity of the programmer over speed and performance of the code itself. To some people, this is the wrong tradeoff. To others, Ruby and the design principles behind it are the epitome of what programming should be about: joy in creating software.

Birth of Ruby

Ruby was born from Matz's love of programming. When Matz was in junior high, his father brought home a pocket computer that ran the computer programming language BASIC. BASIC, or the Beginner's All-purpose Symbolic Instruction Code, was a general-purpose programming language created in the 1960s. When personal computers such as the Apple II emerged in 1977 (followed by the Commodore 64 in 1982), these early PCs came with BASIC installed. Matz began to program his computer himself and over time developed a passion for computer science.

As a teenager, Matz read about the computer programming language Pascal. The computer he had at home didn't support programming in Pascal, but learning about the language inspired Matz to begin reading books and magazines about programming languages. Through his reading, he became aware of other programming languages such as Lisp and Smalltalk. At age seventeen, he decided he'd like to create his own programming language someday.

In an interview on the Changelog podcast, an interview-based podcast focused on software and technology, Matz said:

> Through reading the books about computer programming languages, I found out every programming language was designed by a human being. We don't know who designed English, nor Japanese, but we have, for example, John McCarthy for Lisp or Alan Kay for Smalltalk.
>
> [Each] programming language was designed by a specific person or a group of people. They had an intention or ideas for their programming languages … Even though I didn't have a chance to program in those programming languages in reality, I was really, really interested in the concept of the programming language.

Years later, on February 24, 1993, Matz began developing the general-purpose programming language we know today as Ruby. His programming language inspirations included Pascal, Lisp, Smalltalk, Ada, and Eiffel. Among other things, Matz liked that Pascal tried to help programmers be effective. He also liked that Lisp was very consistent throughout the language, and that everything was done by combining a small number of concepts. He tried to integrate these aspects of Pascal and Lisp into his new programming language.

Design Ethos

When designing a new programming language, it's important to consider what the programming language will be used for and how the language will be formulated. Matz wanted to build a programming language that felt natural but was complex underneath. This dichotomy, he has often said, mirrors life. (To understand his comparison, consider the human body. We look natural and rather unassuming, and yet when you peel back the layers, there is great complexity within our biological systems.) Matz also wanted to build a language that made programming fun, not frustrating, so that the programmer could focus on the end result instead of small, difficult bits of code.

In an introduction Matz wrote to *Programming Ruby: The Pragmatic Programmers' Guide*, he said:

I believe that the purpose of life is, at least in part, to be happy. Based on this belief, Ruby is designed to make programming not only easy but also fun. It allows you to concentrate on the creative side of programming with less stress.

Another major principle that motivated Matz was the concept of DRY programming. DRY programming is a principle first elaborated on by Dave Thomas and Andy Hunt in their first book, *The Pragmatic Programmer*. DRY stands for "Don't Repeat Yourself," and the broader definition is that every piece of knowledge must have a single, clear representation in a system. The goal of DRY programming is to reduce repetition in code, tests, designs, and documentation.

In summary, Matz wanted to build a fun, natural, and DRY programming language. Accomplishing these goals required a well-thought out approach to the structure, **syntax** (the rules that guide the language's form), and execution of the language.

Technical Decisions

When creating a programming language, the language designer must have an intimate understanding of the technical aspects of programming languages and the merits of each choice they make. In an interview with the Linux Dev Center, an online publication of O'Reilly Media Inc., Matz explained how he approached the high-level technical decisions for his new language. Matz's explanation provides a lot of insight into the inspirations for Ruby's major design characteristics, but it also contains a lot of technical terms that may be challenging for anyone new to programming. The sections following Matz's explanations break down concepts like "scripting language" and "**object-oriented** programming" to make it easier to understand Matz's vision. Matz said:

> Back in 1993, I was talking with a colleague about scripting languages. I was pretty impressed by their power and their possibilities. I felt scripting was the way to go.
>
> As a longtime object-oriented programming fan, it seemed to me that OO programming was very suitable for scripting too. Then I looked around the Net. I found that Perl 5, which had not released yet, was going to implement OO features, but it was not really what I wanted. I gave up on Perl as an object-oriented scripting language.
>
> Then I came across Python. It was an interpretive, object-oriented language.

But I didn't feel like it was a "scripting" language. In addition, it was a hybrid language of procedural programming and object-oriented programming.

I wanted a scripting language that was more powerful than Perl, and more object-oriented than Python. That's why I decided to design my own language.

From Machine Language to Ruby

In the 1940s and 1950s, the first computer programmers entered their programs in machine language by flipping switches or using other mechanisms. This type of programming was a laborious process. It was difficult to test, and it required highly specialized knowledge of the machines and the code.

Over time, computers advanced and computer programming matured in parallel. The invention of the compiler by Grace Hopper, in particular, helped move programming from the realm of machine language to languages with more abstraction. Abstraction, in computer science, means that the languages became less like machine language (series of numbers, such as the ones and zeroes that make up **binary code**) and more like human language (conversational and symbolic). The compiler could take the human-entered symbolic code and translate it into machine language, acting as an intermediary between humans and computers.

These mnemonic-based languages were called **assembly languages**. While assembly languages looked more like English than machine language code did, the code still had a one-to-one relationship with the machine language.

Hopper worked for the Eckert-Mauchly Computer Corporation, where she helped develop the UNIVAC 1 and built the first compiler.

For example, GOTO 10 in assembly language translates directly to 10 1000 0001 0000 in binary code. This one-to-one relationship kept the translation process simple and made the code fast and efficient to run. It wasn't quite as fast as using the machine language itself, due to the translation step, but the slower execution speed was balanced by the increased speed in programming.

(As an analogy, consider what would happen if you invented a new language only your friends knew. It would be easier for your friends to learn your new language if each word translated directly to a known word in English. If your new language was more abstract and didn't translate directly to English words and phrases, it would be much more complex and would take people longer to learn and process.)

However, a major drawback of assembly languages was that programmers still had to create programs specific to the machine they were working with. From the 1960s through the 1980s, when Matz was learning to program, computer science progressed through a third generation of programming languages. The third generation included languages such as COBOL, Fortran, Ada, and C. These languages are high-level languages, which means that they had the advantage of being able to run on different machines. They were more abstract than previous generations of programming languages, and it was easier to build in language features like **loops** and **conditional statements**. (A loop, in computer science, tells a program to repeat a series of instructions until a certain condition is reached. A conditional statement is a feature that tells a program to perform different functions depending on whether a condition evaluates as true or false.)

Many of these third generation programming languages, including C and Fortran, were **compiled languages**. A compiled language is written in code that is translated into machine code before the code is executed. (A computer executes a program when the program is run.)

The opposite of a compiled language is an **interpreted language**. In interpreted languages, an interpreter program translates a program line-by-line when the program is run and executes each command. As you might imagine, running a compiled program tends to be faster and more efficient because the program is already translated to machine code. There are many industries and companies that still use languages like C, Fortran, and COBOL because of their speed and power.

C and Fortran, as well as Java, were also examples of **system programming** languages that allowed programmers to build large, complex applications in a language more enjoyable to work with than an assembly language. According to Stanford computer science professor John Ousterhout in *IEEE Computer* magazine,

> System-programming languages were designed for building data structures and algorithms from scratch, starting from the most primitive computer elements such as words of memory. In contrast, scripting languages are designed for gluing: they assume the existence of a set of powerful components and are intended primarily for connecting components together.

Just as many system-programming languages are also compiled languages, many scripting languages, including Ruby, are also interpreted languages. Scripting languages first appeared in the 1960s. Many are still commonly used today including, JavaScript, PHP, Python, and of course Ruby.

Object-Oriented Programming

Matz also specified that he wanted his language to be an object-oriented language, or one in which programmers build programs that rely on manipulating data structures (called **objects**) with defined functions that can be applied to those objects.

Objects, in computer programming, are chunks of data that have both a state and a behavior. As an analogy, if a bicycle is an "object," its "state" could be "two wheels" and its behavior could be "rolling forward." **Methods**, which are similar to functions in other languages, can be applied to a bicycle, like "roll" and "brake" and "park."

Ruby is completely object oriented, which means that everything in Ruby is an object. This is a key differentiator of Ruby from other object-oriented languages like Python, which are not 100 percent object oriented.

The opposite approach to object-oriented programming is called procedural programming, in which programmers design programs around series of functions (actions) that manipulate data. Fortran, COBOL, BASIC, Pascal, and C are all procedural programming languages. The modern language Go, published in 2009, is also a procedural programming language.

In the early 1990s, there was no 100 percent object-oriented scripting language that satisfied Matz. He turned his dissatisfaction into an opportunity to fulfill his childhood dream of creating a programming language by creating Ruby.

Initial Release

By August of 1993, Matz had accomplished the first "Hello, World!" program in Ruby. Running a "hello, world" program is a traditional way that programmers show that something (in this case, a programming language) they have built works as intended. It is a kind of tradition in computer science that this program is written to display the message "hello, world."

That summer, Matz also settled on the name Ruby. He had built Ruby in part to improve on and replace a programming language named Perl, and he liked the idea of giving his new language another gem name. On a symbolic level, rubies are beautiful and valuable, which is a nice connotation for a new invention. On a practical level, the word "ruby" is well known, short, and easy to type.

In December of 1994, Matz put the Ruby source code (program instructions in their raw form) on the internet. He had gained a lot of knowledge by reading the source code of other software on the internet, and he wanted to give back to the greater community by putting his own code for Ruby up on the internet for others to read. He also created a mailing list for people interested in Ruby. Within two weeks, the mailing list had two hundred members. At the time, Matz was surprised that so many people were interested in a new language from an unknown programmer.

In his interview on the Changelog podcast, Matz said, "Ruby is designed after my preference or tastes. Surprisingly, so many other people felt a similar way toward programming and programming languages. That kind of preference inspired them to get involved in the Ruby community."

At the time, Matz assumed that Ruby would face the fate of many other programming languages. People would play with it like a toy, he thought. Like toys do, it would lose its popularity over time and eventually disappear. He was very, very wrong.

Matz

○ ○ ○

Yukihiro "Matz" Matsumoto grew up in Yonago in the Tottori Prefecture in Japan. (Prefectures are administrative divisions in Japan, like states in the United States or provinces in Canada.) Tottori is the least populated prefecture in Japan, and it has both oceans and mountains.

Matz became interested in computer programming as a teenager and studied computer science at Tsukuba University. He has worked as a computer programmer ever since. In 1993, Matz created his most significant career contribution, Ruby. In an interview with the website Artima, Matz described Ruby's biggest difference from other programming languages:

> Language designers want to design the perfect language. They want to be able to say, "My language is perfect. It can do everything." But it's just plain impossible to design a perfect language, because there are two ways to look at a language. One way is by looking at what can be done with that language. The other is by looking at how we feel using that language—how we feel while programming ...
>
> Instead of emphasizing the what, I want to emphasize the how part: how we feel while programming. That's Ruby's main difference from other language designs. I emphasize the feeling, in particular, how I feel using Ruby. I didn't work hard to make Ruby perfect for everyone, because you feel differently from me. No language can be perfect for

everyone. I tried to make Ruby perfect for me, but maybe it's not perfect for you. The perfect language for Guido van Rossum is probably Python.

Guido van Rossum is the creator of Python, so let's hope he agrees!

In addition to creating Ruby, Matz has released other open-source products including cmail, an Emacs-based email user agent. (Emacs is a text editor where programmers write their code.) He also wrote *Ruby in a Nutshell*, a practical Ruby reference guide first published in 2001.

Today, Matz lives in Matsue City in the Shimane Prefecture of Japan, not far from his childhood home. In 2011, Matz became the Chief Architect of Ruby at Heroku, a San Francisco-based company that provides a popular platform for **deploying** and running web apps.

Heroku supports many languages, but it supported only Ruby applications when it was founded in 2007. The name Heroku, in fact, is a combination of the English word "heroic" and the Japanese word "haiku" in a nod to Matz and the Japanese roots of Ruby. Matz's responsibilities there are to work along with a core team of Rubyists on developing new features and enhancements for the Ruby programming language.

In 2011, Matz won the Award for the Advancement of Free Software from the Free Software Foundation. The award recognizes individuals who have made great contributions to the progress and development of free software.

Initial Reception

Ruby's first public release was in December of 1995. After releasing the first version, Matz worked alone on developing the Ruby language until 1996. At that point, a greater programming community began to form around the language, and other programmers began to contribute to developing and improving the language.

Matz first publicized Ruby in English in 1998 through an English-language mailing list. This was the language's first significant introduction to non-Japanese speakers. Within a few years, there were English-language books about Ruby including Matz's own book *Ruby in a Nutshell*.

In 2000, Ruby gained a strong validation when the well-known programmers and authors Dave Thomas and Andrew Hunt wrote a book on Ruby called *Programming Ruby: A Pragmatic Programmer's Guide*. (Thomas and Hunt have written a number of books under their own publishing imprint, The Pragmatic Bookshelf, which strives to help programmers grow their knowledge and skills.) Ruby, it seemed, was not just a toy.

In 2001, the first Ruby conference, or RubyConf, was held in Tampa, Florida, and had about thirty attendees. By the mid-2000s, Ruby had gained mass acceptance in part due to the introduction of **Ruby on Rails**, a **framework** for web development. Today, programmers around the world use Ruby, and RubyConf draws hundreds of attendees (over 650 people in 2016).

Ruby on Rails

Ruby is a general-purpose programming language, which means that it can be used for a variety of purposes including statistical analysis and programming hardware devices. Today, however, it's most famous for its use in web development. This fame is largely due to the invention of Ruby on Rails, a framework used to make it easier to build websites with Ruby. (Web frameworks simplify web development by providing a default infrastructure for the standard components of a web application.)

The Birth of Ruby on Rails

The Rails framework was invented by David Heinemeier Hansson in 2003. Hansson, popularly known by his internet handle DHH, worked at a Chicago-based software company called 37signals. At the time, 37signals was a consultancy that provided web design services to clients.

In 2003, Hansson began building a web-based project management tool called Basecamp that the company could use to manage its client work. Hansson had been working on client projects primarily in PHP and, less frequently, in Java. Though he enjoyed the end result of programming, he did not enjoy the act of programming in either PHP or Java. When it came time to begin developing Basecamp, Hansson chose a language he was newly acquainted with and excited about: Ruby.

According to Hansson in an interview with the Changelog podcast:

> Here was a programming language that took such a radically different approach to what is a programming language. It redefined the question for me. Programming language was no longer just about how do you make the bits and the bops go in the right order. It was about "How does the programmer feel about it?" That to me was such a huge breath of fresh air.

Prior to this time, very few people were using Ruby to build web apps and the language wasn't optimized for web development. Hansson realized that in the course of building the Basecamp application, he had made a number of tools that could be used to make it easier to build any web application. He felt confident others would prefer to use those tools rather than choose all the details from scratch for a new web app—especially if they were on a tight deadline. Inspired by this idea, he extracted the Rails framework from the Basecamp app and made it available as open-source software.

In general, Rails is a tool that creates the framework of a web application with many default values that are chosen by experienced web developers as the best tools for the job. In more specific terms, the Rails framework provides default structures for a web application's database, web server, and web pages to make it easier to get a web application up and running.

To understand the function and value of Rails, imagine going to a restaurant that offers a pre-set multicourse menu. The courses are selected for you by the chef, who has considered the choices carefully and picked what works well together. However, if you don't eat meat, you might ask for a vegetable soup instead of a meat-based version for the soup course.

Similarly, in Rails, many choices are already made for the web developer but the web developer can swap out a default menu option if they prefer another choice. Rails establishes the infrastructure a web developer needs to build a web app (as a chef does when she decides a pre-set dinner menu will have a soup course, an entrée, a side dish, and dessert), and establishes conventions that make it easy to get started

(like establishing that miso soup is the default soup in that dinner menu.)

In "The Rails Doctrine," Hansson expands on this dinner menu analogy to emphasize the value of preset configurations:

> How do you know what to order in a restaurant when you don't know what's good? Well, if you let the chef choose, you can probably assume a good meal, even before you know what "good" is … [This is a] way to eat well that requires you neither be an expert in the cuisine nor blessed with blind luck at picking in the dark …
>
> With Rails we decided to diminish one good, a programmer's individual privilege to choose each tool in their box, for a greater one: a better toolbox for all. The dividends are legion.

While individual freedom to choose the best tool for the job is valuable, so too is having a framework that makes it easy to get started without having expert knowledge about each decision point.

The first public release of Rails, Rails .05, was on July 24, 2004. To market Rails, Hansson created a demo video in which he built a blog engine in fifteen minutes to demonstrate the value of Rails. The blog engine video has become somewhat of a legend in Rails history, as it was a straightforward marketing approach that successfully showed programmers just how powerful Rails could be.

Rails's Design

Like a building has an architecture that contains its basement, floors, exterior walls, plumbing, wiring, and more, software applications also have an architecture. In software, however, the "architecture" describes different software components and how they are connected.

Rails uses an architecture known as **model-view-controller (MVC)** architecture. In an application with MVC architecture, the model is the realm of the application that contains all of the application logic, or the rules of the program, and it is mapped to a database filled with information. (When a programmer writes the code for a program, they create that application logic.) The controller takes user requests and determines which file should be shown to the user through the user interface, known as the view. The user makes requests such as to see information stored in the database (such as viewing an available hotel room on a booking app) and makes other types of requests that modify information stored in the database (such as booking a hotel room, which means the database must reflect that room's new booking.)

Rails is designed with two major philosophies. The first is DRY, or "Don't Repeat Yourself." The second is "Convention over Configuration" which means that most choices are made using established conventions. Configuration is only necessary when special circumstances mean the established convention is not adequate for the web app.

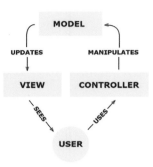

The MVC architecture is used in several languages including Ruby, Java, C#, and PHP.

Like Ruby, Rails is open-source software, which means it is free to use, repurpose, and distribute.

How Rails Affected Ruby

Rails had a strong impact on the Ruby community. Prior to Rails, Ruby was a new language that some programmers enjoyed using. After Rails, Ruby was a major player in the web development world. Using Ruby in conjunction with the Rails framework allows programmers to write more code in fewer steps compared to the older, more widely used Java programming language. It also allows programmers to rapidly prototype much faster than with Java. The ability to quickly build and test an app is immensely valuable to startups.

By 2006, three years after Ruby on Rails was released, Ruby had gained mass acceptance in the programming world. In many polls, Ruby is one of the ten most-popular programming languages. There are many software companies that use Ruby, software-consulting companies that specialize in building applications in Ruby on Rails, and many conferences dedicated to the worlds of Ruby and Ruby on Rails.

Today, the development and direction of Rails is led by the Rails core team, a group of contributors that develop major new features and handle complaints.

Ruby's Evolution

Before creating Rails, Hansson worked primarily in PHP as a contract software developer.

Over time, Ruby has matured and gained new features within the language itself, as well as new frameworks and tools designed for Ruby developers.

New Versions

Ruby was first released as version 0.95 in 1995, and the language has been in use for over two decades. Ruby, as a

David Heinemeier Hansson

○ ○ ○

David Heinemeier Hansson was born in 1979 in Copenhagen, Denmark. His first introduction to business was selling pirated CDs (compact disks) as a young teenager. "That was sort of the beginning I think, which is not necessarily a very glorious career but it got me started to thinking just about moving a product and getting people to buy it," Hansson said in an interview with Jaime Tardy of the Eventual Millionaire podcast.

Hansson attended the Copenhagen Business School and earned a bachelor's degree in computer science and business administration. He started working at a software consulting company named 37signals in Chicago as a Denmark-based contractor. (Contractors are not employees and don't have the typical benefits like health insurance or retirement plans. In return, they have more flexibility to negotiate rates, location, and other details of their relationship to a company.) In 2005, Hansson joined the 37signals staff in Chicago to concentrate on Basecamp. In 2014, 37signals rebranded from a consultancy into a product company named Basecamp. Basecamp has been very successful, and Hansson and his Basecamp co-founder Jason Fried have chosen to continue leading the company and improving the product instead of selling or taking on outside investors.

Hansson is the co-author of several books on business. The first book, titled *REWORK*, is a playbook for building a business. The second book, *REMOTE: Office Not Required*, explores the trend of working from home, while a third book, *Getting Real*, details 37signal's approach to software design. All three of these books were co-authored by his Basecamp co-founder Fried, and *REWORK* became a New York Times bestseller. Hansson also co-wrote *Agile Web Development with Rails*, part of the Pragmatic Programmers series.

In his spare time, Hansson races cars in the FIA World Endurance Championship. In 2014, he and his Danish co-drivers Kristian Poulsen and Nicki Thiim won the GTE AM class in the 24 Hours of Le Mans, the world's oldest, active, sports-car endurance race. That same year, the team won the FIA World Endurance Championships.

Overall, Hansson has started in thirty-six races, won six, and won the championship once. In an interview with the Slashdot website, he described racing as similar to programming:

> Driving a race car fast is surprisingly similar to programming software. And managing and influencing a race team is incredibly similar to managing a software team. It's all systems theory. What are your positive feedback loops? What are the constraints you have to exploit? Same with developing a feel for grip. It's like developing an eye for good software. You get a sense of quality that's embedded in your gut feeling when you get good enough that you can just make the right calls most of the time without too much deliberation. It's a great feeling.

Hansson has a wife and two children. In 2005, Hansson won Best Hacker of the Year at OSCON, the O'Reilly Open Source Convention, for creating Rails.

language, has gained sophistication and new features through updates and new versions. Initially, new stable versions (versions that were well tested and considered "final" for that version) were released in quick succession. For example, Ruby went from version 1.0 in December of 1996 to Ruby 1.6 in September 2000, just four years later. However, moving from Ruby 1.6 to Ruby 1.8 (the next stable version) took three years.

New Tools

Over the past two decades, Ruby programmers have also gained new tools to use when working with Ruby, such as new web frameworks. Rails is still the most popular framework used for Ruby web developers, but there are many other options to choose from. The most popular choice after Rails is Sinatra.

Rails is a model-view-controller web framework with many conventions that are designed to make web developers more efficient. It's easy to get from installing Rails to having a basic Rails page. From there, however, there is a fair amount of complexity in creating a Rails app, and some people dislike the amount of set conventions that come with the Rails framework.

Sinatra, meanwhile, is a more minimalist framework, with an emphasis on simplicity and flexibility. It does not require the same model-view-controller structure that Rails does. Generally, Sinatra is considered best suited for small projects while Rails is the better choice for larger applications. Other minimalist alternative to Rails are **micro frameworks** like Grape and the small, fast Cuba. (A micro framework is essentially a term for "minimalist framework" and indicates a framework has more flexibility and fewer set conventions.)

There are many more tools beyond frameworks designed to improve the process of building apps in Ruby. If you're interested in following the latest news, Reddit and HackerNews are common areas where programming tools and services are discussed.

```ruby
                if @last_col == 0
                    col = ( @lines[ row ] =~ /\S/ )
                else
                    col = 0
                end
            #when Diakonos::BOL_ALT_FIRST_CHAR
            else
                first_char_col = ( ( @lines[ row ] =~ /\S/ ) or 0 )
                if @last_col == first_char_col
                    col = 0
                else
```

```ruby
    end

    def cursorToBOL
        row = @last_row
        case @settings[ "bol_behaviour" ]
            when Diakonos::BOL_ZERO
                col = 0
            when Diakonos::BOL_FIRST_CHAR
                col = ( ( @lines[ row ] =~ /\S/ ) or 0 )
            when Diakonos::BOL_ALT_ZERO
                if @last_col == 0
                    col = ( @lines[ row ] =~ /\S/ )
                else
                    col = 0
                end
            #when Diakonos::BOL_ALT_FIRST_CHAR
            else
                first_char_col = ( ( @lines[ row ] =~ /\S/ ) or 0 )
                if @last_col == first_char_col
                    col = 0
                else
```

```ruby
    end

    def cursorToBOL
        row = @last_row
        case @settings[ "bol_behaviour" ]
            when Diakonos::BOL_ZERO
                col = 0
            when Diakonos::BOL_FIRST_CHAR
                col = ( ( @lines[ row ] =~ /\S/ ) or 0 )
            when Diakonos::BOL_ALT_ZERO
                if @last_col == 0
                    col = ( @lines[ row ] =~ /\S/ )
```

How It Works

In this chapter, we'll look at what you need to be able to program in Ruby, how Ruby is translated into machine code, what Ruby code looks like, and examples of common products that are built using Ruby. This chapter is not intended to be a guide to programming in Ruby, and any descriptions of syntax will be brief. It will, however, give you a better idea of what is involved in programming with Ruby and what you might do with it.

Opposite: Diakonos is an example of a text editor. A text editor is one of the few tools you need before getting started on coding projects.

Required Tools

There are only a few tools needed to program in Ruby. First, you need a computer with Ruby installed. If your computer has a Linux or Mac operating system, Ruby may already be installed on your computer. If not, or if you want to be sure you have the very latest stable version, it's very simple to install it.

The process differs based on your operating system, and the most up-to-date instructions for each operating system are described on the official Ruby programming language website, www.ruby-lang.org.

You'll also need a text editor program such as Sublime Text in order to create plain text files that contain Ruby code. These files are saved to directories on the computer and accessed from the terminal program when it comes time to run a Ruby program. Sublime Text is a very popular text editor. Other common text editors include Vim and Emacs. Ultimately, it's up to the individual programmer to choose the text editor they like working with best.

You can also use an IDE (integrated development environment) instead of a text editor. IDEs provide more features than text editors, such as automatic code completion or the ability to restore previous versions of code. It's less common to use an IDE than a text editor, but one of the more popular IDEs in the Ruby community is RubyMine.

The Ruby Interpreter

Programming languages are made up of two primary components. The first is the language **specification**, which provides definitions for what a programming language looks like and how it is used. The second is a program that translates that language into something the computer can understand.

Some programming languages, such as Python, have a formal language specification document that states what the language looks like, what it can do, and how it is used. Ruby does not currently have an official specification document. In cases like this, the specification is provided indirectly by example in a reference implementation of the language. (Other programmers can refer to this implementation to see how the language works.)

The Ruby interpreter is the program that translates Ruby code into instructions the computer can understand. When you install Ruby, you are actually installing the Ruby interpreter.

Matz wrote the Ruby interpreter in C, a language that was first developed by Dennis Ritchie between

Bell Laboratories researchers developed technology including the laser, the transistor, the Unix operating system, and the programming languages of C and C++.

1969 and 1973 at the mid-century American innovation hub called Bell Laboratories.

What exactly does the Ruby interpreter do? First, it breaks Ruby code down into chunks called tokens. For example, if a line of code says "a + b" the tokens would be ["a", "+", "b"].

The tokens are tagged with metadata that defines what the tokens are, such as whether a token is an integer or a string of text or an operator (like the + in the example above). These tokens are arranged into a structure called an abstract syntax tree and then compiled into **bytecode** that is run on the Ruby **virtual machine** and executed. (A virtual machine is a program that imitates a computer, and Ruby bytecode is the machine language of the Ruby virtual machine. Other virtual machines have their own specific bytecode machine language.)

The interpreter Matz built, also called Matz's Ruby Interpreter (MRI) or CRuby, is the reference implementation of the Ruby programming language. This is the interpreter that Matz and the core team update and expand with each release of Ruby. A programming language can have more than one implementation, however, as sometimes other programmers want to use the same language specification but interpret or compile the code in a different way.

One example of an alternative Ruby implementation is JRuby. JRuby allows programmers to write Ruby code that can run on the **Java Virtual Machine (JVM)**. For a language to run on the JVM, it must first be compiled into Java bytecode, which is the machine language of the JVM. JRuby has a slow startup time and consumes a lot of computer memory, but the JVM runs code faster than the Ruby interpreter. Once JRuby is started, JRuby is typically much faster at executing code than the standard Ruby interpretation.

Another advantage of JRuby is that a programmer can use Ruby code in places where Ruby wouldn't normally work, so long as Java can run in that environment. For example, JRuby makes it possible to use Ruby code to build a program for an Android phone. It also gives programmers the ability to use

Java **libraries** (programs or pieces of programs that can be re-used in other applications).

Another alternative Ruby implementation is the mruby interpreter, which Matz himself designed as a lightweight version of Ruby. The mruby interpreter is useful for programming **embedded systems**: computer systems completely contained within a piece of hardware or machinery, such as cell phones, smart thermostats, and self-driving vehicles.

Embedded systems are usually designed for a specific task and have significant resource constraints. Specifically, embedded systems typically have less memory

The Nest thermostat is an example of a smart device with a sophisticated embedded system. It learns your schedule to automatically adjust the temperature.

and **CPU** (**central processing unit**, or the "brain" of the computer that executes instructions) available to run programs. At the same time, embedded systems typically operate in devices we expect to run very quickly. We want our thermostats and cell phones to respond immediately to our inputs, and we certainly expect self-driving cars to respond instantaneously to obstacles. Thus, when picking a language for an

Object-Oriented Code

○ ○ ○

As mentioned in the previous chapter, Ruby is an object-oriented programming language, which means that the code is centered around data. Take a look around you. All of the people and objects you see could be represented as objects in a Ruby program. For example, if someone wrote an application that tracked which students were present at school each day, students would be objects in the program. Other objects in the program might include classrooms and teachers.

In Ruby, each object belongs belong to a **class**. Programmers can create classes, define class variables and class methods that objects of the class can have, and create new objects within that class. For example, the class "Student" could have class variables that represent student name and student ID number.

A characteristic of object-oriented code is that when a programmer wants to invoke or "call" a method for a variable or specific instance of an object, the method is connected to the variable or object instance using **dot notation**.

For example, in a program with an existing class called Student, typing Student.new calls (uses) the .new method to create a new object belonging to class Student. If the class Student has class variables of name and ID number, the new object could be created with those variables defined by writing Student.new("Melinda", 3313).

embedded system program, the language itself must use minimal computing resources, run very fast, and be able to accomplish the tasks at hand.

C and C++ are two of the most common languages used for embedded systems because both languages consume relatively little memory and run very quickly. The traditional Ruby interpreter (Matz's Ruby Interpreter) on the other hand, consumes a significant amount of memory and runs less quickly. Thus, the streamlined mruby interpreter provides a better way for programmers to use Ruby when they want to build programs that work for embedded systems.

Many factors make Ruby so desirable that programmers create various implementations of it instead of just switching languages. For many programmers, Ruby's high-level, scripting, object-oriented syntax is greatly preferred to programming in less abstract, system-programming languages like C and Java.

Ruby Syntax

An important part of both designing a new programming language and learning a new programming language is understanding its syntax. (As you'll recall, these are the rules that guide a language's form.) Matz wanted to create a language that felt natural, like a spoken or written English conversation. The naturalness of Ruby is evident because when you read Ruby code, even if you don't know the language well, you can get an idea of what the code is saying.

For example, if you wanted to tell a program to print the word "Cats!" three times, you would write the following code:

```
3.times { print 'cats!' }
```

When you ran your program, you would get the following result:

```
cats!cats!cats!
```

This is a simple example, of course, but it is easy to read the line of code and understand what it will do. You are telling the program to "three times, print the words 'cats!'" And that is what happened. In this way, Ruby looks and feels natural to the programmer.

Most programs are much more complex than that, and they require many different types of objects and actions. They can be harder to read, but with effort and practice, the code will become easier and easier to read until it is clear as a sentence in a book.

A Sample Program

The best way to learn what the syntax of a programming language looks like is to read a lot of code. Let's look at a longer example from a real application. The following code is part of an application built using Ruby on Rails called Spot Us. Spot Us was a web app that allowed users to hire freelance journalists. (It has since shut down.) The code below shows what happens when a user tries to post a comment on Spot Us.

First, simply read through the code and see what makes sense. Perhaps you can see which message appears when a comment is saved and which message appears when an error occurs during posting? What happens if someone isn't logged in and tries to post a comment? Then continue reading and refer back to this sample program as syntax elements are discussed.

```
class CommentsController <
ApplicationController
      skip_before_filter :verify_authenticity_token
      before_filter :login_required

      bounce_bots :send_bots, :comment, :blog_
url
```

```
resources_controller_for :comments, :only
=> [:create, :index]

response_for :create do |format|
  format.html do
    if resource_saved?
      flash[:notice] = "Successfully
created comment"
      redirect_to :back
    Else
      flash[:error] = "An error occurred while
trying to post your comment."
      redirect_to enclosing_resource
    End
  End
End

response_for :index do |format|
  format.any do
    redirect_to(enclosing_resource)
  End
End

Protected
```

```ruby
def send_bots
  redirect_to root_path
End


def can_create?
  if current_user.nil?
    store_comment_for_non_logged_in_user
    render :partial => "sessions/header_form"
and return false
  End


  access_denied unless current_user
End


def new_resource
  returning resource_service.
new(params[resource_name]) do |resource|
    resource.user = current_user
  End
End


def resource_service
  if enclosing_resource
    enclosing_resource.comments
```

```
    Else
        Comment
    End
  End


  End
```

We'll refer back to this small program while exploring some of the different parts of Ruby syntax. Keep in mind the following overview is purposely brief and high-level. It is intended to show what the code looks like and to discuss some of the most important elements of how Ruby performs actions. The following sections will cover objects, a few common data types, variables (names for objects), and methods (essentially the verb that determines what actions take place).

Strings

A string is any sequence of characters surrounded by single or double quotation marks. "asld#%!gas" is a string. So is "I love Lucy." and '13326236'.

In the code sample above, "An error occurred while trying to post your comment." is a string. The text within the double quotes appears on the screen if an error occurs when a user tries to post a comment.

When a string is surrounded by single quotation marks, the characters within the single quotes are the literal characters shown to the user, with a few small exceptions.

When a string is surrounded by double quotation marks, Ruby does more processing on the content of the string and sometimes the characters shown in the code will be slightly different than the characters shown to the user. For example, if a string within a set of double quotation marks has a backlash character, such as \n, Ruby will do something based on that backslash character. In the case of \n, Ruby forces a line break at that spot. For example, look at the following code:

```
puts "Roses are red, \n Violets are blue"
```

This code would return two lines:

Roses are red,
Violets are blue

Integers

Integers are numbers. There are no numbers in the above code sample, but we saw the integer 3 earlier in this chapter in the example of 3.times { print 'cats!' }.

To visually break up very large numbers, such as 1,000,0000, we use underscores instead of commas.

For example, 1000000 can also be written as 1_000_000 to make it easier to read the number.

Boolean Values

If you've ever looked for a book in a library database program, you may have used Boolean logic such as "AND," "OR," or "NOT." These Boolean operators tell the search program what logic to apply to the search results. For example, a search for "magic AND wizards NOT game" would help you find information about magic done by wizards, excluding results related to the trading card game known as Magic: The Gathering or games played by the basketball team the Washington Wizards.

Ruby also uses Boolean logic expressions as a core part of computation. "And," "or," and "not" are the three fundamental Boolean operators in Ruby. These operators can be evaluated using the values "true," "false," or "nil." True and false are self-explanatory. For example, if a function checks whether an entered value is greater than 5, either the value is greater than 5 (true) or it is not (false). The operator "nil" represents nothing, or the absence of any value. Anything that is not false or nil, in Ruby, is considered to be true.

In the sample program, we saw an example of a Boolean value when the program checked to see whether or not the user was logged in before posting a comment:

```
def can_create?
  if current_user.nil?
    store_comment_for_non_logged_in_user
    render :partial => "sessions/header_form"
and return false
  End
  access_denied unless current_user
End
```

The program checks to see whether or not the user can create a program based on whether the user is logged in or not. If the value of current_user is nil, the user must first log in to use the commenting feature.

Other Data Types

In addition to strings, integers, and Boolean values, there are many other data types in Ruby that are very useful for storing information. Other common data types include symbols, ranges, arrays, and hashes. You'll learn more about these data types and many more in courses on Ruby programming.

Variables and Constants

In Ruby, variables and constants are used to refer to objects. Variables are lower-case words and are temporary in nature. Their meaning can change throughout a program. Constants, meanwhile, are capitalized words that, like proper nouns, are more permanent. Minnesota, for example, is the name of a state and thus a proper noun. It's unlikely that Minnesota's state name will ever change. Likewise, once a constant is assigned a value it typically keeps that value throughout a program.

Methods

Methods are like the verbs of Ruby code. Methods are actions attached to variables and constants. In the program above, we see several instances of methods, including in the following lines of code:

```
def can_create?
  if current_user.nil?
    store_comment_for_non_logged_in_user
    render :partial => "sessions/header_form"
and return false
  End
```

```
access_denied unless current_user
End
```

The keyword def defines a method called can_create? The statements between def and the final End define what the method does. The can_create method defined here checks whether the current user is logged in and denies access for users who are not.

Operators

In Ruby, expressions are calculated or compared using operators. Examples of operators include:

- +, − (plus and minus)
- *, / (multiply and divide)
- defined? (checks if a symbol is defined)

Keywords

Ruby uses certain words to control the logic of an expression, such as:

- if
- and
- do
- else

- elseif
- next
- unless
- until

In the code sample above, we see if and else used here:

```
response_for :create do |format|
  format.html do
    if resource_saved?
      flash[:notice] = "Successfully created comment"
      redirect_to :back
    else
      flash[:error] = "An error occurred while trying to post your comment."
      redirect_to enclosing_resource
    end
  end
end
```

The keywords if and else tell the program what to do. If the comment is saved, then the user gets a success message. Otherwise, (else), the user gets an error message.

SketchUp Ruby API

○ ○ ○

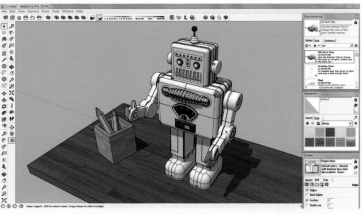

In 2017, SketchUp debuted a SketchUp for Schools program to bring 3D modeling tools to K–12 students.

SketchUp is a 3D modeling program that makes it easy for users to turn two-dimensional drawings into modifiable three-dimensional models. It's a useful tool for a variety of users, from architects and interior designers to computer game designers and people using 3D printing to create products.

In SketchUp, users begin by drawing two-dimensional shapes such as circles and rectangles as well as lines in a program that looks similar to Paint or Adobe Illustrator. A "push/pull" tool lets users pull on the shapes and lines to create three-dimensional shapes and then push and pull the three-dimensional shape to change its dimensions.

By combining simple lines and shapes, users can create sophisticated three-dimensional models in the program. As an example, an architect might create a three-dimensional model of a house she is designing. After creating the basic shapes of the house in three dimensions, she can navigate around her modeled house to view it from different angles and distances.

SketchUp wasn't built using Ruby, but the SketchUp Ruby **API** allows Ruby programmers to expand on the core capabilities of SketchUp. (An API is an **application programming interface**. APIs provide a way for applications to integrate and send data back and forth.) If a programmer wants custom drawing tools or animations, for example, they can write a SketchUp Ruby Plugin, which is a Ruby text file that integrates with SketchUp via the SketchUp Ruby API.

Former designer and current SketchUp Extensibility Product Manager Chris Fullmer wrote about his introduction to the SketchUp Ruby API:

> I had spent a few hours learning some basic Ruby syntax, then I dove into the SketchUp Ruby API with the express purpose of being able to pushpull more than one face at a time—a task repeated so regularly in the City Planning office I was working at, where I created model after model of countless cities across the country. I couldn't believe how amazing it was that I could transform a task that can be so time-consuming in SketchUp into a few simple lines of code that execute instantly. I saved myself days of double-clicking, pushpull, carpal-tunnel-laden time. NO, I saved my company days of time. What?! Give that man a raise!

SketchUp Ruby API
(continued)

○ ○ ○

The code Fullmer used (shared on the SketchUp Developer site) looked like this:

```
model = Sketchup.active_model
selection = model.selection.to_a
faces = selection.grep(Sketchup: :Face)

faces.each do |face|
    face.pushpull(rand(20))
end
```

We can see here what Fullmer did: using a few lines of Ruby code in a SketchUp Ruby API script, each face was pushpulled. Fullmer was able to make a three-dimensional modeling process do an action in bulk that he had been doing by hand (or by mouse!) one at a time, repeatedly. Note that the .to_a method is a method that has since been deprecated (retired) that was previously used to convert objects to arrays.

Learning More About Ruby Syntax

The aim of the tour of the Ruby language syntax outlined above is to introduce you to what Ruby code looks like and how it operates. The entirety of Ruby syntax is much more complex than described in this book. Different approaches to fully learning Ruby are discussed in the final chapter of this book, and there are resources for getting started listed in the Further Information section at the back of this book.

Everyday Applications

The most common daily application of Ruby is web development as part of Ruby on Rails.

Everyday Public Use

Most people interact with Ruby on a regular or semiregular basis when they use popular web applications such as Airbnb to find a vacation rental home or Square to pay for coffee at a coffee shop.

Here's a brief list of other popular web applications that use Ruby:

- Kickstarter, the crowdfunding site for entrepreneurial or community-minded ventures
- Hulu, the online video-streaming service

- Bleacher Report, the sports news site
- Goodreads, the site for tracking progress in book reading, as well as book reviews and recommendations

Consumers of these products aren't exposed to the Ruby code when they use them, but they are interacting with Ruby nonetheless.

Everyday Developer Use

Many web developers interact with Ruby on a daily basis by working with products such as GitHub and Heroku. GitHub is a tool that allows programmers to store their application source code and manage different versions of that code. For example, when building a new feature,

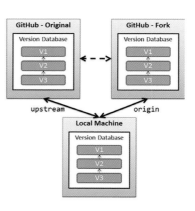

This diagram shows using "upstream" to retrieve code from its original repository and "origin" to pull and push code to a forked repository.

developers create a copy of the current production code and build the new feature in a nonproduction environment. If something goes wrong, the live product remains stable, and the stable code is

Hulu's video streaming website and several of its services are built using Ruby on Rails.

preserved. Later, the new code can be merged with the production environment code so that the new feature is live. GitHub also allows programmers to collaborate with others on their projects and track bug reports and feature requests. GitHub hosts applications written in many languages, but GitHub itself was written in Ruby.

Heroku is a "platform-as-a-service" or PaaS. It is a cloud-based platform that allows developers to deploy and run apps. Deployment is, at a high level, the process of taking an application's source code and turning it into an app available on the internet and ready for use. Heroku supports many languages, but it too was built in Ruby.

<Chapter Three/>

Strengths and Weaknesses

R uby is a popular programming language, especially for web development. It is elegant and has qualities of natural language that make it easy to learn, read, and write. It also has its drawbacks, however, namely that it is slower than many other languages.

Strengths

Ruby has many strengths, largely based around the happiness of programmers and the active, positive Ruby community.

Opposite: Ruby has user groups in the United States and around the world that meet to share ideas and learn.

Matz has said it's important to focus on humans when programming, as humans are the ones who program and use computer software.

Programmer Happiness

One of the groundbreaking aspects of Ruby is its focus on programmer happiness. Though Matz said his original inspiration was simply to have fun while designing the language, that focus on fun in design translated into the language itself. Ruby became a language centered on programmer joy and happiness, a language that prioritized the human instead of the computer. This wasn't a common idea in computer programming languages at the time, making Ruby somewhat revolutionary.

Community

The focus on programmer happiness helped create another major strength of Ruby: its community. Ruby grew in popularity much faster than Matz expected. After Rails was released, the community grew even more. There are many free tools to get started learning Ruby and Rails, including online books and tutorials.

The community's focus on open source means that there is a big community of people collaborating together, and that the community is structured around the value of helping others and improving shared resources.

RubyGems

Because Ruby is open source, Ruby programmers are able to contribute to the growth and expansion of the Ruby language. One way to do this is by creating a **gem** and adding it to **RubyGems**.

A gem is the name for a Ruby library. Turning frequently used code into a library is more efficient than writing the same code in its entirety every time. When Ruby programmers create a chunk of code that will have value to others, they can turn it into a gem. RubyGems is a packaging system that programmers can use to create, share, and install gems.

RubyGems is a built-in part of Ruby. You can browse through available gems by going to www.rubygems.org. However, gems are installed through the **command line** (a user interface that lets you control your computer or a program via text instructions) using the code: gem install #type gem name here.

An example of a very popular gem is Rails. That's right—Rails, the framework that makes it easy to do web development in Ruby, is a software library. To install Rails, you type:

```
gem install rails
```

To install a specific version of Rails, or another library, you write --version. For example:

```
gem install rails --version 5.0.
```

The most popular gem of all time is not actually Rails but a tool called Bundler. Bundler makes sure that Ruby projects have all of the exact gems and correct versions that they need. Software projects often include many different libraries that, over time, have new updates and licenses. That creates a **dependency**, or a reliance on an external library for a program to work properly. Most programs have many dependencies, and because libraries can be nested within other libraries, the dependencies can be essentially hidden from the developer. Without a tool like Bundler, programmers are likely to run into dependency issues, or conflicts due to out-of-date versions or other issues.

Ease

Ruby is generally considered an easy language to learn, and especially an easy language to read because of how closely the syntax mirrors natural conversation. It's especially easy if you have a good grasp of the English language. Many of the built-in methods are English words, and if you're trying to do a common procedure, the name of the method is likely very intuitive and descriptive. While other languages may strive to do the same, Ruby is known for being especially close to natural English language.

Fast Prototyping

As discussed earlier, a major benefit of Ruby when used in conjunction with the Rails framework is the speed at which programmers can build and deploy a prototype. This development speed makes Ruby on Rails popular in the startup world, where time is of the essence. Startups need to be able to quickly put an idea out in front of the market, validate if their idea works (or pivot to a new idea), and then improve on that idea. Ruby on Rails makes this possible in a way that languages like Java do not.

Ruby on Rails co-founder David Heinemeier Hansson famously demonstrated the speed of building an app in Ruby with a YouTube video of how to build a blog engine in fifteen minutes. (In web developer lingo, building an app is sometimes called "spinning up an app.") He typed in the Rails command and generated a bunch of primarily empty files and a Ruby server. This small bit of marketing sparked interest in Ruby on Rails, because it showed the big value proposition of the framework—ease and speed of web application development.

Hardware Programming

Ruby can be used to program hardware systems such as Arduino boards and Raspberry Pi to create do-it-yourself projects and prototype new ideas. An Arduino board is an electronics board with a microprocessor that can run one program at a time. The Arduino can read inputs, such as perceiving light on a sensor or a finger on a button, and create a corresponding output such as activating a motor or turning on an LED. Arduino boards are popular with hardware hacking enthusiasts because the software and hardware are open source (they can be used and modified for any purpose, including commercial gain) and they are inexpensive.

In one real-life example, a man used an Arduino board to create an analog speedometer for his bike (most bike speedometers are digital, and show speeds in numerical format such as 17 mph). He used the Arduino to measure the time it took the wheel to complete one revolution using a magnet and a sensor. The Arduino then uses that input to calculate and display the speed in miles per hour. He then used the Arduino to control a servo motor, which has gears and a shaft, to move a needle over an analog speedometer display.

Ruby is also installed by default on the Raspberry Pi, a microcomputer the size of a credit card with USB ports that can connect to mice, keyboards, and other hardware pieces. The Raspberry Pi can be used in electronics projects, like building a motion-activated music speaker. The makers of Raspberry Pi created the small, cheap computer to encourage kids and adults to learn programming and creative hardware skills.

Programmers can use a Ruby gem called Serial Port to communucate with an Arduino through the board's serial port, a basic communication interface.

A Ruby micro framework called Artoo has been designed specifically to make it easier for programmers to write Ruby code for robotics and hardware. Artoo was inspired by the Sinatra web development framework but was optimized to work on embedded systems including the Raspberry Pi, Arduino, and other hardware and robotics platforms such as the Roomba vacuum cleaner and Pebble smart watch.

Duck Typing

Ruby uses a style of programming known as duck typing. If you have ever heard the phrase "If it walks like a duck and talks like a duck, it must be a duck," you have a basic understanding of duck typing. In Ruby, if an object in code behaves like a certain kind of object, it can pass as that type of object. (Even if it isn't.)

According to the authors of *Programming Ruby: The Pragmatic Programmers' Guide*:

> Now, it seems like folks react to this in two ways. Some like the kind of flexibility and feel comfortable writing code with dynamically typed variables and methods … Some, though, get nervous when they think about all those objects floating around unconstrained. If you're coming to Ruby from a language such as C# or Java, where you're used to giving all your variables and methods a type, you may feel that Ruby is just too sloppy to use to write "real" applications.
>
> It isn't.

Raspberry Pi has sold more than 12.5 million units, making it the best-selling British computer in history.

As the authors note, duck typing makes Ruby fast and flexible to code in. The interpreter is, in a sense, generous. It tries to interpret the code as usefully as it can instead of throwing errors if an object isn't precisely the object that it expects. This convenience can be an asset for prototyping quickly.

Some programmers feel that the ambiguity introduced by duck typing can also be a weakness in some cases. They prefer the rigidity of a language like Scala for bigger, more complex programs because that rigidity enforces discipline and consistency across the app and between programmers. And yet, there are many large applications that use duck typing without running into significant type-related issues, as the Pragmatic Programmers authors note. They explain:

If you use a variable for some purpose, the chances are very good that you'll be using it for the same purpose when you access it again three lines later. The kind of chaos that could happen just doesn't happen.

On top of that, folks who code Ruby a lot tend to adopt a certain style of coding. They write lots of short methods and tend to test as they go along. The short methods mean that the scope of most variables is limited: there just isn't that much time for things to go wrong with their type. And testing catches the silly errors when they happen.

Weaknesses

Ruby's weaknesses are largely related to its performance and technical capabilities.

Performance

A famous example used when critiquing Ruby's performance is Twitter's move away from Ruby on Rails in 2010. Twitter, first launched in 2006, was originally built on Ruby on Rails. By 2010, the app had so many users tweeting from around the world that the site was crashing regularly.

Twitter's engineers knew they needed to make a change, and they rebuilt the app using (for the most part) the programming language Scala. Scala is a general-purpose, functional programming language that is compiled to Java bytecode, the code that runs on the JVM.

The JVM is known for speed and efficiency. The JVM originally only ran Java, but today, it can run a variety of languages including Scala and Clojure. (In addition to Scala, Twitter is now built using a little of Clojure and Java as well.) The JVM is very good at handling something Ruby lacks: **concurrency**.

Concurrency

In life, two or more separate things often happen in parallel, like when a school has a softball game in progress while a track and field meet takes place nearby. The two events are happening independently of one another, but in parallel.

Parallelism is everywhere in our daily life and the same is true for computers. When you're at your computer, you likely have many **processes** (independent sets of instructions) running at once. Perhaps you're streaming music while messaging with your friends and playing a game. Your computer has to handle all of these processes at once and make sure it has enough resources available to do so.

Ruby on Rails and Ajax

○ ○ ○

Ruby on Rails is useful for quickly building a web application, and many large companies like Airbnb and Groupon rely on Rails for their popular, heavily trafficked apps. Many companies choose to use JavaScript in some form (such as jQuery, Ajax, AngularJS, BackboneJS, or EmberJS) to make their website look more modern.

To understand the difference between an application with JavaScript and an application without, consider an app that showcases pets available for adoption. The app, when built purely using Ruby on Rails without JavaScript, contains the necessary information such as a homepage with listings of various animals and a page for each of those animals.

Consider the following two common user behaviors:

- Clicking a button to load more available pets on the homepage
- Posting a comment on a specific dog's page to ask if the dog is good with kids

As a Ruby on Rails app without any JavaScript mixed in, the pages are likely very static and not especially interactive. Doing either of the actions listed above sends a request to the server, the server handles the request (such as by storing the new comment or by retrieving more data), and sends the request (either the new comment or additional data) back to the browser. The page must reload entirely before the user can either view more pet listings on the home page or see their comment added to the dog's listing.

This is called a synchronous request, and it's not particularly user-friendly or quick to reload the page every time it's updated. Ideally, the following behaviors correspond to the following responses from the browser:

- Clicking a button to load more available pets on the homepage causes the browser to quickly and elegantly pull in more listings of available pets without reloading the page.
- Posting a comment on a specific dog's page to ask if the dog is good with kids causes the new comment to appear below existing comments without reloading the page.

We can use an asynchronous request, more commonly called an Ajax request, to process these actions and achieve the desired outcomes. (Ajax stands for Asynchronous JavaScript and XML.)

An Ajax request allows a browser to request data from a server, process the response, and update the page without fully reloading that page. In the case of adding a comment asking if a dog is good with kids, the server creates the comment and generates JavaScript to add the comment to the existing comment list. It sends that JavaScript to the browser, the browser evaluates the new JavaScript behind the scenes, and the browser dynamically updates the page without reloading it.

If this dynamic, elegant behavior sounds obvious to you, it's because it's a standard component of modern web application design. Users expect apps that dynamically respond to their actions, and Ajax is one of the technologies that makes this behavior possible.

In computer science, there is a difference between parallelism (when two processes take place at the same time using different allocated resources, such as by using a multicore processor) and concurrency (when two processes or **threads** appear to happen at the same time but are actually taking turns using shared resources, such as on a single-core machine). Concurrency, when done well, looks like parallelism—but it's a challenge.

Most software programs are written sequentially such that one instruction is completed at a time. In order to run two processes at the same time, computer programs can either run two processes in parallel by creating separate threads (independent, scheduled sequences of instructions) and running them at the same time. Parallelism takes up more memory and computer resources than running one thread at a time.

In some cases, there aren't enough resources for parallelism to be possible. Additionally, the parallel programs will likely need to be able to talk back and forth, which creates additional programming complexity. Therefore, as an alternative, computer programmers can **interleave** threads to achieve concurrency, or to make it seem like both are happening at once. This saves on memory and resource usage.

To interleave tasks is to divide processes into smaller chunks and alternate between them to create

Quack Like Ruby, Bark Like C

○ ○ ○

Let's look at how to write a small program to print (display) text in Ruby compared to how you would write a program in C to do the same thing. We'll use Ruby to print the word "Quack!" five times and C to print the word "Bark!" five times.

In Ruby, the code is:

```ruby
class Duck
    def initialize(number_of_quacks:)
      @number_of_quacks = number_of_quacks
    End

    def quack!
      @number_of_quacks.times do
        puts "Quack!"
      End
    End
End


duck = Duck.new(number_of_quacks: 5)


duck.quack!


#> Quack!
```

Quack Like Ruby, Bark Like C
(continued)

○ ○ ○

#> Quack!

#> Quack!

#> Quack!

#> Quack!

In C, the code for the same function (using dogs and barks instead of ducks and quacks) is:

```
#include <stdio.h>

    int main(void) {
      int number_of_barks = 5;

      for(int i=0;i<number_of_barks;i++) {
        printf("Woof!\n");
      }

      return 0;
    }
```

While the C code looks less like English, the terms aren't entirely impossible to decipher, and its logic is straightforward. In fact, it looks similar to a mathematics problem and its meaning can be generally understood using the rules of mathematics and logic. C is a procedural programming language (instead of object-oriented), which means that C programs specify a series of steps and procedures written in specific structure.

Dennis Ritchie, creator of C

The Ruby code, on the other hand, uses English terms to tell the computer what to do. Many programmers prefer Ruby's ease of use, while others prefer C's speed and performance.

an illusion that both processes are happening at once. As an analogy, consider training for a mathematics competition. Instead of studying one subject in entirety before moving on to the next subject, you could study a little algebra, followed by a little geometry, followed by a little trigonometry and then repeat the process. In doing so, you would be interleaving the subjects in your study process.

If you could switch between subjects at a rate of fractions of a second, you'd create an illusion that you are studying all of the subjects simultaneously. This is approximately how computer programs handle concurrency—by interleaving tasks and switching quickly between them to create an illusion that they are all happening at once.

Writing computer programs that can handle concurrency is much harder than writing a simple sequential program. Programmers must ensure that the different threads efficiently use shared resources and that concurrent processes don't end up in **race conditions**.

A race condition occurs when two different threads try to modify shared data at the same time, such as in a hotel room reservation example. Imagine this: Customer A's reservation attempt triggers an availability check and finds that room 201 is open. Customer B's reservation attempt triggers an availability check and finds that room 201 is open. The reservation system successfully books room 201 for customer B. The reservation system attempts to book room 201 for customer A, but the room is no longer available due to the interleaved processes. A race condition has been created, and an error occurs for customer A.

As you may imagine, writing programs with multiple threads and making sure they interleave at the appropriate time and that data is locked (prevented from being modified) when under active modification by a process can be difficult and frustrating.

Other programming languages, like Scala and Clojure, have come up with a new model of asynchronous concurrency that resolves these headaches. Essentially, a program is divided into different processes and threads and each is sent off to perform their instructions. They come back and coordinate when finished. This is much more straightforward than the interwoven dance of concurrency and multithreading performed in Ruby.

Ruby does not include standard libraries to support asynchronous concurrency, and for many programmers, this is a major disadvantage to programming with Ruby over a language like Scala or Clojure.

Limitations

Ruby is a general-purpose programming language, but it is not an all-purpose programming language. It is a great choice for web application development, especially for startups that need to rapidly prototype their product. It is not a good choice if you want to build iPhone or Android apps, for example. Android applications are typically built using Java, and iOS applications are primarily built using Objective-C.

Ruby can be used to build games for mobile devices and personal computers (there's an example of a successful game built using Ruby in the next chapter!), but it is not the ideal programming language for game development. Better languages from a performance perspective are C++ or Java. C++ is the most common language used to build video game engines because, while a difficult language to learn, it gives the programmer better control over the actual hardware, and the code can run very quickly. That said, while many programmers heatedly debate the best programming language to use in game development, others counter that the best language to build a game in is the language you like enough to stick with.

JavaScript is a better language than Ruby for making beautiful web **front ends**. That leads to the next section: JavaScript can be used in conjunction with Ruby on Rails to create web applications with a strong **back end** and a beautiful front end. If you are going to learn Ruby, especially Ruby on Rails, it is useful to also learn JavaScript or to work on a team that integrates Ruby on Rails and JavaScript to build web applications.

Professional programmers rarely know just a single language. It's generally beneficial to know several languages and technologies and to know how to pick the best tool for each job. The next chapter will cover how to get started learning Ruby, the complementary technologies used in web development, and the prospects for a professional Ruby programmer.

<Chapter Four/>

Getting Started with Ruby

One of the core benefits of Ruby is that it is supposed to be fun for programmers to use. Don't mistake that for being easy to learn, however. Ruby is complex and requires dedicated study and practice to develop the skills necessary to build production-ready apps and to hone the skills needed to join a professional team of developers.

How to Learn Ruby

There are many different ways to learn programming languages, including Ruby. Some of the major differences between methodologies include:

Opposite: Learning to code in an educational setting is just one option. Some programmers opt to teach themselves to code.

- Financial cost
- Timelines
- Accountability and support
- Qualifications of instructors
- Depth of instruction
- Delivery of instruction

For some people, limiting financial cost is the most important factor in their decision. For others, it may be more important to achieve programming proficiency as quickly as possible, but they also need the support of peers to help them to stay motivated. And for others, a classroom environment with access to trained instructors might be the way they learn best.

There is no single best way to learn, just a way that works best for each individual student. Some methods, however, might regularly produce better outcomes or completion rates, and those are important factors to include in the decision. This section will go over each of the primary ways to learn to program and the different qualities of each option.

Self-Guided

One low-cost way to learn to program is to pursue a self-guided education using books on programming, tutorials, and other resources that are available on the internet.

Why's Poignant Guide to Ruby is part graphic novel, part quirky narrative, and part Ruby tutorial.

Popular books on Ruby include:

- *Learn Ruby the Hard Way*
- *Programming Ruby: The Pragmatic Programmers' Guide*
- *The Well-Grounded Rubyist*

Popular free Ruby tutorials include:

- Code School's "Try Ruby" tutorial
- RubyMonk
- Learn Ruby the Hard Way

This option allows students to learn at their own pace and in their own way. However, there is little accountability because there are no deadlines, instructors, or fellow students who can help motivate you or require students to make progress.

Free Online Courses

A number of companies provide free online courses (sometimes called MOOCs, or Massive Open Online Courses) that students can enroll in. Coursera is one such company. Not all courses at Coursera are free, but many are. Some courses have an option for paying for a completion certificate after finishing a course.

The courses are structured similarly to taking an online course at a university. There are video lectures, homework assignments, quizzes, and class discussions. The course takes place over a specific date range, and there are deadlines for assignment and quiz completion.

Free online courses offer zero financial commitment, flexibility to study from home, and more structured timelines than pure self-study. Typically, the courses are designed by professors from accredited universities across the United States.

However, studies have shown that when students have no financial commitment to an educational program, they're less likely to complete that program.

It seems that having some money at stake makes people more likely to complete a program and get their money's worth.

According to edX, a competitor to Coursera, their students are ten times more likely to complete a course if they sign up for the paid version with a verified certificate than if they take the free version of the same course.

Paid Online Courses

There are also a number of programming education companies that provide online programming courses for a fee. Udacity, for example, is a Silicon Valley–based company that provides a variety of "nanodegrees" that students can enroll in for a monthly fee.

Like a free online course at Coursera, Udacity's model offers a way for students to learn to program at home with lectures and assignments and support from instructors and fellow students. The timelines provide momentum. While not free, courses such as those provided by Udacity are much cheaper than many other paid options such as a boot camp or a traditional college degree.

Other companies that provide online programming education for a fee include Codecademy and Code

School. Both Codecademy and Code School provide free tutorials as well.

Programming Boot Camps

Developer or coding boot camps are a newer model for learning to program. Typically, boot camps offer a way to learn programming skills in a condensed period of time. Instruction is primarily delivered on site, and students pay thousands of dollars to attend the boot camp. They typically also have to temporarily relocate to attend the boot camp for a period of some months.

Developer boot camps vary in qualifications, of course, such as instructors, cost, course length, skills taught, post-graduation employment rates, and much more. Because they are a newer model of education, those interested in a boot camp should research various options thoroughly. In many cases, especially due to the expense and the lack of accredited degree, boot camps are best for professionals who already have career experience, want to pivot to a new career path, and can set aside the money and time to learn to code in a rather intense format.

Dev Bootcamp was the first of its kind and opened in 2012. It taught **full-stack** web development curriculum, including Ruby on Rails as well as front-end development, and database systems such as SQL and PostgreSQL. It also included a weeklong career training component. Since then, numerous other bootcamps have emulated and expanded on Dev Bootcamp's model. (Dev Bootcamp closed in 2017.)

Another boot camp with courses in Ruby on Rails is the Flatiron School in New York City. The Flatiron School offers a fifteen-week, full-stack web development program that costs $15,000 as of March 2017. Around 95 percent of graduates had technical jobs within 120 days of completing the program.

Certificate Programs

Many community colleges offer nondegree certificates in web development. These certificate programs are not the equivalent to a four-year degree, but they offer a way to show to an employer that a student has successfully completed courses in web design at an accredited educational institution. The courses are typically taught by experienced instructors (or industry professionals) in a classroom with graded assignments. Because it's not a four-year college degree, it's a cheaper way to learn in a traditional education environment. Not all certificate programs include programming-intensive courses, or offer Ruby programming courses, however.

Computer Science Degrees

A four-year bachelor's of science degree is the most time-intensive and expensive way to learn to program (though scholarships may ease the cost or eliminate expenses entirely). A four-year degree in computer science offers the benefits of learning from highly educated and trained professors and access to all of the support and resources that universities can provide in terms of tutors, professor office hours, and career

Stanford (*left*) and MIT (*right*) both teach web application computer science courses with topics such as concurrency and security.

guidance. It also provides a thorough education in the fundamentals of computer science and related disciplines, such as courses on:

- Various computer programming languages
- Advanced mathematics
- Algorithms
- Data science
- Cryptography
- Hardware and devices

Some organizations require that job applicants have a bachelor's degree (or higher) for all or specific roles, however. If you are considering a career in software development, a traditional university degree is the most comprehensive education path you can choose and will make you a strong candidate for a wide variety of roles. If you plan to start a software company, it can also be advantageous to take business classes or even double-major in business while at a university.

Careers in Ruby

According to a report by Burning Glass Technologies, based on job postings advertised in 2014, Ruby is among the fourteen best programming languages to learn when considering salary and job openings.

Ruby had fewer job postings than the other thirteen top programming languages in the report with 16,492 jobs posted. In comparison, there were 86,688 jobs posted for PHP developers, 387,433 jobs

A Dark Room

○ ○ ○

A unique use of Ruby is the text-based role-playing game (RPG) named *A Dark Room*. Programmer Michael Townsend originally built *A Dark Room* in 2013. In its original form, the game was web-based, designed to be left open in the web browser and played throughout the day.

A Dark Room was praised by gaming critics for its suspense and intrigue.

The web-based version is very simple. In the beginning, there are two lines of black text on a white background ("the room is freezing" and "the fire is dead") and a button that says "stoke fire." Stoking the fire advances the story with additional lines of text. Eventually, a small counter begins tallying how many stores of wood the player has left. As the game advances, strangers appear, the wood stores dwindle, and the player must make decisions about what to do next.

Another software developer, Amir Rajan, found the game and asked Townsend if he could adapt the game for Apple's iOS devices (including the iPhone and iPad). At first, Rajan tried building a mobile version of *A Dark Room* in Objective-C, the programming language Apple uses for iOS devices.

The work was laborious, and Rajan switched to RubyMotion, an implementation of the Ruby programming language that makes it simple to build apps for iOS (iPhones and iPads), watchOS (Apple Watch), OS X (Apple computers), and Android (phones, tablets, TVs, and more). RubyMotion is especially helpful for developers who already use Ruby because it allows them to build apps for mobile devices without having to learn Objective-C or Swift to program on Apple devices or Java for Android devices.

In a case study on *A Dark Room*, Rajan said:

> I refactored often, and what I found was that Objective-C and OCUnit just made that an utter chore. I had a copy of RubyMotion, I knew that it had an RSpec-style testing framework, and I knew how easy it was to refactor Ruby code. So I put the Objective-C version of *A Dark Room* aside and fired up RubyMotion.

Rajan released the iOS version of *A Dark Room* in late 2013. At first, it had about one thousand downloads a month at a cost of $0.99 per download. In April 2014, however, sales spiked to hundreds per day, and the game became the most-downloaded game on the United Kingdom App Store; it eventually reached the top of all downloads in the United States App Store. It stayed there for the remainder of the month.

Rajan did not get rich off the downloads of *A Dark Room*, by any means. The average app in the App Store costs $0.99, like *A Dark Room*, and the average revenue (money the developer gets to keep) per download from the App Store is $0.10.

posted for Java developers, and 131,748 jobs posted for Python developers.

However, Ruby had the highest average annual salary at $107,547. In comparison, the annual average salary was $104,228 for Python developers, $99,104 for Java developers, and $88,087 for PHP developers.

Initial salaries, of course, will be lower than the average salary for a given career. Pay varies by region, but a 2015 report found that graduates of the Flatiron School's boot camp started at an average salary of $74,447. This is much higher than the average salary in the United States, across all jobs, of $44,569 (based on Social Security Administration data from 2014).

Complementary Technologies

When you learn to proficiently read, write, and understand a new language like Spanish or Arabic, you can use that language to converse with others who speak the same language you do. You can order from menus and navigate new environments and, aside from cultural differences, dialects, and slang, your new language skills will generally suffice.

This isn't generally true for learning a new programming language like Ruby. There are many aspects to building a computer program and knowing a general-purpose language like Ruby isn't enough to achieve strategic goals.

For example, Airbnb uses Ruby on Rails, but not exclusively. There are a number of other languages and technologies used in the web development and design process to create a highly performative and modern final product.

The single most common technology to learn in conjunction with Ruby is the Rails web development framework. This book has described Rails in great detail in previous sections, but let's look a little closer at what it is at its core: Ruby on Rails is designed as a full-stack framework (which means it includes everything you need to build a full web application), but it is strongest as a web application's back end paired with additional programming languages to create the web app's front end.

Back and Front

A web application's back end consists of the server, an application, and a database. It is the part of the application the application user doesn't see, but it's where all of the information and processing power comes from. Ruby, along with Python and PHP, is a common choice for building a web application's back end.

A web application front end, on the other hand, is the portion of the app that the user can see and interact with. A front end consists of both the web design and the front-end web development. Web design, strictly speaking, can be completed in a program like Adobe Illustrator without ever touching code. While web design doesn't necessarily require programming skills, incorporating web design is a crucial part of building an app that looks good and appeals to users. A graphic designer who doesn't code, for example, might produce rough sketches of a web app (called a **mockup**) and higher fidelity (more accurate) Adobe Illustrator files that show what the web application will look like when it's completed. If the graphic designer doesn't program, these files are handed off to a person who does know code to implement the design.

The person who implements that design is doing front-end development. Front-end development includes a combination of **HTML** and **CSS** as well as languages such as JavaScript.

HTML, an acronym for Hypertext Markup Language, is used to format text and graphics on web pages. For example, if you were writing a WordPress blog post about your family's camping trip and chose to use the HTML editor to format your post, you could type "I <b>literally</b> couldn't handle the mosquitoes!" The <b> and </b> are HTML tags that indicate that, in the published post, you want the

Pair programming is common in the Ruby world. It's a good way for programmers to teach each other and to spot mistakes.

sentence to look like: "I **literally** couldn't handle the mosquitos!" HTML tags are used to create headings (like newspaper headlines), subheadings, italicized text, linked text, bullets, numbered lists, and much more.

CSS is an acronym for Cascading Style Sheets, which are a set of rules that tell a web browser how to display a document written in HTML. HTML can handle simple effects like bold and italicized font, as described above, but it doesn't produce the level of polish that can be achieved using CSS.

CSS rules are made of two components, a set of properties and a selector. The properties describe values such as "I want to make everything tagged as Element A have dark gray font on a white background with five pixels of empty space around the text." The selector determines what element you want to apply that set of properties to, such as all of the body paragraphs in your web page.

The JavaScript programming language has many uses beyond front-end development, but when paired with Ruby, it's often for front-end development in the form of jQuery or AngularJS or BackboneJS. The previous chapter included an example of using Ajax to improve the design and functionality of a website. Ajax isn't its own programming language, but Ajax requests are written in JavaScript.

A popular JavaScript library that makes it easier to find and select elements on a page is jQuery. It creates interactive page elements and animations and handles events like a user clicking on a link. Most Ruby on Rails programmers will need to use jQuery at some point in the web development process.

AngularJS and BackboneJS are both JavaScript-based front-end web application frameworks used to build very fast web pages. Choosing a framework like AngularJS or BackboneJS for a Ruby on Rails app's front end can be useful because it means that each side of the app is built using tools selected for the precise development purpose at hand. Separating front-end and back-end development also means that the front-end developers can build the front end of the app, going through rapid phases of prototyping, while the back-end developers are building the back end of the application. When both sides are ready, they're merged.

A Bright Future for Ruby

Matz and the Ruby core team are continuously working to improve Ruby by making it faster, more powerful, and more enjoyable to use. According to a keynote conference talk Matz gave at RubyConf 2016, he doesn't want new versions of Ruby to be drastically different than previous versions because he doesn't want to break compatibility with previous versions and discourage adoption. At the same time, it's important to him that the language continue to move forward so that it doesn't lose users and become obsolete over time.

Ruby is a standard language to learn for any programmer interested in web application development. There are many programming languages that are faster than Ruby or that are better suited to specific purposes, but Ruby is an easy first programming language to learn. Its beginner-friendly nature coupled with its usefulness in web application development helps Ruby thrive.

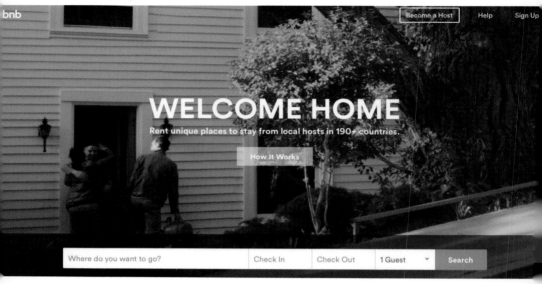

Companies like Airbnb rely on Ruby on Rails, and it doesn't look like that will change any time soon!

Many companies use Ruby in conjunction with Rails because they are a useful language and framework for quickly building and launching a web application. Once a Ruby application is launched, it's easy to improve and expand the application. The ease of programming in Ruby also makes it a popular choice at many companies, as developers enjoy using a language that feels closer to English and less like computer language.

Ruby has an active core development team working to make the language stronger, faster, and more enjoyable for programmers to use. In addition, many

Ruby programmers continue to make open-source contributions to Ruby and Ruby on Rails to improve existing Ruby libraries and create new libraries that make a Ruby developer's work a little easier. Between the core team and open-source contributions, Ruby will continue to grow, improve, and evolve for many years to come.

application programming interface (API) A set of specifications that define how applications integrate and communicate.

assembly language A low-level, symbolic programming language that typically has a one-to-one relationship to machine language.

back end The behind-the-scenes components of an application, including the application itself, a database, and a server.

binary code A programming language that uses only 1s and 0s or another two-symbol system.

bytecode Code that is typically processed by a virtual machine rather than a hardware computer.

Cascading Style Sheets (CSS) A set of rules that tells a web browser how to display a document written in HTML.

central processing unit (CPU) The brain of a computer that carries out program instructions.

class A high-level grouping of objects, often with defined variables and methods.

command line A text interface where users can enter text commands to interact with and modify computer files.

compiled language A programming language that is translated into machine language before runtime.

concurrency When two processes run at the same time using a shared resource.

conditional statements If-then statements in which an outcome happens if a condition is true.

dependency A reliance on an external software library for a program to work properly.

deploy To make program code or code that changes an existing program publicly available as an application.

dot notation A format used to invoke a method in Ruby in which an object or variable is on the left of the dot and a method is on the right side, such as student.new.

embedded system A computer system embedded in a device, such as in a smartphone or smart thermostat.

framework A tool that simplifies web development by providing a default infrastructure for the standard components of a web application.

front end The components of an application that a user sees, typically built with HTML, CSS, and JavaScript.

full-stack Development that includes everything necessary to build a full web application, from the database and server to JavaScript for the user interface.

gem The name for a Ruby software library.

HTML A markup language used to format text and graphics on web pages, such as bold or italicized font.

interleave To split two or more programs or threads into smaller chunks that alternate running.

interpreted language A programming language that is translated line-by-line at runtime.

Java Virtual Machine (JVM) A virtual machine that runs Java programs, as well as programs written in languages that compile to Java bytecode such as Scala, Clojure, and Haskell.

library Pre-written code that can be added to a program to make development faster or simpler.

loop A block of code that repeats until a certain condition is met.

method Code that bundles a series of statements into a single unit.

micro framework A minimalist web development framework with more flexibility and fewer set conventions than a traditional framework.

model-view-controller (MVC) An infrastructure for building applications consisting of business logic (the model), user request handling (the controller), and showing information to a user (the view).

object A data structure that can have methods and properties; the building blocks of Ruby code.

object-oriented A style of programming that is centered around objects and data instead of procedures and logic.

parallelism When two processes take place at the same time using different allocated resources.

processes In computing, a process is a unit of execution; a single process can contain multiple threads.

race condition A condition that occurs when two different threads try to modify shared data at the same time.

Ruby on Rails A web development framework that makes it easier to build websites with Ruby.

syntax The rules that guide a language's form.

system programming Programming languages designed for building data structures and algorithms from the lowest-level elements of computers, such as memory.

thread Independent, scheduled sequences of instructions.

virtual machine A program that imitates a computer and can free a programmer from having to satisfy actual computer requirements in designing a program.

Books

Cooper, Peter. *Beginning Ruby: From Novice to Professional.* New York: Apress, 2009.

Pine, Chris. *Learn to Program.* 2nd Edition. Raleigh, NC: The Pragmatic Bookshelf, 2009.

Seibel, Peter. *Coders at Work: Reflections on the Craft of Programming.* New York: Apress, 2009.

Websites

Getting Started with Ruby on Rails

https://www.codeschool.com/learn/ruby

Explore free courses on Code School's website.

Ruby Rogues

https://devchat.tv/ruby-rogues/page/16

Learn about Ruby programming and get insight on tools and methodologies through interviews with notable Ruby programmers on this podcast.

Why's Poignant Guide to Ruby

http://poignant.guide/book/chapter-1.html

Learn the basics of Ruby through this quirky, illustrated, online book.

Videos

"Ruby vs. Python: Choosing Your First Programming Language"

https://www.youtube.com/watch?v=b48XWPTbapA

Ben Neely discusses the similarities and dissimilarities between Ruby and Python and gives an overview of the history and uses of Ruby on Rails.

"Useing You're Type's Good [sic]"

https://www.destroyallsoftware.com/talks/useing-youre-types-good

A humorous (and intentionally mistitled) walkthrough of dynamic versus static typing by Gary Bernhardt, a frequent speaker on Ruby and programming.

Beck, Kent, et al. "Manifesto for Agile Software Development."
Agile Alliance, February, 2001. https://www.agilealliance.
org/agile101/the-agile-manifesto/.

Brooks, Ashley. "14 Best Programming Languages Based on
Earnings & Opportunities." Rasmussen College, May 4,
2015. http://www.rasmussen.edu/degrees/technology/
blog/best-programming-languages-based-on-earnings-and-
opportunities/.

Cplusplus.com. "Structure of a Program." Retrieved May 12,
2017. http://www.cplusplus.com/doc/tutorial/program_
structure/.

Fairhurst, Gorry. "Example of Assembly." Retrieved May 15,
2017. http://www.erg.abdn.ac.uk/users/gorry/eg2069/
assembly.html.

Fullmer, Chris. "Welcome!" SketchUp Developer. Retrieved
May 12, 2017. http://developer.sketchup.com/en/content/
welcome.

Heinemeier Hansson, David. "David Heinemeier Hansson."
Retrieved May 12, 2017. http://david.heinemeierhansson.
com/.

———. "Rails is omakase." December 27, 2012. http://david.
heinemeierhansson.com/2012/rails-is-omakase.html.

———. "The Rails Doctrine." Rails, January 2016. http://rubyonrails.org/doctrine/.

Horne, Starr. "How Ruby Interprets and Runs Your Programs." November 3, 2015. http://blog.honeybadger.io/how-ruby-interprets-and-runs-your-programs/.

Kehoe, Daniel. "What Is Ruby on Rails?" October 11, 2013. http://railsapps.github.io/what-is-ruby-rails.html.

Krill, Paul. "Ruby Pioneers Come Clean on the Language's Shortcomings." *InfoWorld*, January 16, 2015. http://www.infoworld.com/article/2870966/ruby/ruby-pioneers-come-clean-on-languages-shortcomings.html.

Louis, Tristan. "How Much Do Average Apps Make?" *Forbes*, August 10, 2013. https://www.forbes.com/sites/tristanlouis/2013/08/10/how-much-do-average-apps-make/.

Martsoukous, George. "An Introduction to AJAX for Front-End Designers." Tutsplus, February 2, 2016. https://webdesign.tutsplus.com/tutorials/an-introduction-to-ajax-for-front-end-designers--cms-25099.

Matsumoto, Yukihiro. "RubyConf 2016 – Opening Keynote." Confreaks.TV, 2016. http://confreaks.tv/videos/rubyconf2016-opening-keynote.

Metz, Cade. "The Second Coming of Java: A Relic Returns to Rule Web." *Wired*, September 25, 2013. https://www.wired.com/2013/09/the-second-coming-of-java/.

Oracle. "What Is an Object?" Retrieved May 11, 2017. https://docs.oracle.com/javase/tutorial/java/concepts/object.html.

Ruby. "About Ruby." Retrieved May 11, 2017. https://www.ruby-lang.org/en/about/.

RubyMotion. "RubyMotion Success Story: A Dark Room." April 8, 2014. http://www.rubymotion.com/news/2014/04/08/rubymotion-success-story-a-dark-room.html.

Slashdot. "The Slashdot Interview with Ruby on Rails Creator David Heinemeier Hansson." August 31, 2016. https://interviews.slashdot.org/story/16/08/30/1759216/the-slashdot-interview-with-ruby-on-rails-creator-david-heinemeier-hansson.

Stacoviak, Adam, Jerod Santo, and David Heinemeier Hansson. "10+ Years of Rails." Podcast. *The Changelog*, March 6, 2015.

Stacoviak, Adam, Jerod Santo, and Yukihiro Matsumoto. "23 Years of Ruby." Podcast. *The Changelog*, May 7, 2016.

Stewart, Bruce. "An Interview with the Creator of Ruby." O'Reilly Linux Dev Center, November 29, 2001. http://www.linuxdevcenter.com/pub/a/linux/2001/11/29/ruby.html.

Storimer, Jesse. "Does the GIL Make Your Ruby Code Thread-Safe?" Ruby Inside, June 19, 2013. http://www.rubyinside.com/does-the-gil-make-your-ruby-code-thread-safe-6051.html.

Tardy, Jaime. "Millionaire Story David Heinemeier Hansson."
The Eventual Millionaire, Retrieved May 12, 2017.
http://eventualmillionaire.com/millionaire-story-david-
heinemeier-hansson/.

Thomas, Dave, Chad Fowler, and Andy Hunt. *Programming
Ruby: The Pragmatic Programmers' Guide*, Second Edition.
Raleigh, NC: The Pragmatic Bookshelf, 2004.

Thomsen, Michael. "A Dark Room: The Best-Selling Game That
No One Can Explain." *New Yorker*, June 11, 2014. http://
www.newyorker.com/tech/elements/a-dark-room-the-
best-selling-game-that-no-one-can-explain.

Toal, Ray. "Introduction to Concurrency." Retrieved May 12,
2017. http://cs.lmu.edu/~ray/notes/introconcurrency/.

Wilcox, Ryan. "The Many Interpreters and Runtimes of the
Ruby Programming Language." Toptal. Retrieved May 12,
2017. https://www.toptal.com/ruby/the-many-shades-of-
the-ruby-programming-language.

Venners, Bill. "The Philosophy of Ruby." Artima Developer,
September 29, 2003. http://www.artima.com/intv/ruby.
html.

Page numbers in **boldface** are illustrations. Entries in **boldface** are glossary terms.

Rachel Keranen is a writer based in Minneapolis, Minnesota. Her work focuses on science, software, and entrepreneurship. She's passionate about learning and loves taking deep dives into science and history. In addition to the books that she writes for Cavendish Square, such as *The Power of Python* and *The Composition of the Universe: The Evolution of Stars and Galaxies*, Keranen's previous work includes articles in the *Minneapolis/St. Paul Business Journal* and the *London Business Matters* magazine. Keranen enjoys traveling, biking, and spending time near water.